Good and True
Some Questions Tell Their Own Lies

**a play and a radio play
by Stan's Cafe**

ISBN 978-1-913185-11-4

Published by Stan's Cafe
Birmingham, UK
2020

www.stanscafe.co.uk

Good and True © Stan's Cafe 2000
Some Questions Tell Their Own Lies © Stan's Cafe 1998
Photos © Ed Dimsdale 2000
Publication © Stan's Cafe 2020

Contents:

Good and True   1
Bonus Material
Original Programme Notes   50
Some Questions Tell Their Own Lies   52

Good and True

Joanne

[N, C & A are in the room drinking tea. N is eating a banana. C leaves the room and returns dragging S on, he arranges her as if she has fallen over. N hands C the banana's skin which is placed within the accident scene]

C   Oh dear, oh dear. Come on love, are you alright?
Wake up.
That's it, nice and easy.
You took a nasty fall there didn't you.
A   Crashing.
C   Can you see me?
S   Yes.
C   How many fingers am I holding up?
S   Two.
C   Excellent!
A   You were lucky, you could have caught your head on the edge of the table.
N   Oh look, here's the culprit *[picking up banana skin]*.
C   Oh another of those, they're lethal.
A   If I had a pound for every one of those!
S   Who are you?
C   Do you think you can make it to the chair?
S   Yes.
C   Well done, upsy daisy, great.
S   Where am I?
A   Take a seat.
S   What time is it?
[C looks to a watch he is not wearing]
C   We won't keep you long.
A   We've got to ask you some questions but first we need your name.
S   Jane.
C   Jane, are you sure?
A   I don't think it is, is it?
N   I don't like it.
A   No.

C	Something else?
S	Um, Jo, Joanne?
A	Joanne?
N	Nice.
C	Excellent!
N	Joanne.
A	Joanne what?
S	Yes.
C	What?
S	Yes.
A	Sorry, Joanne, what's your surname?
	[There follows an improvisation around the confusion between Watt and what]
S	You see, Watt is my name.
A	Yep, yep, we're with you now, sorry about that.
C	Haven't you ever thought of changing it? Your name.
S	No, why should I?
C	To clear up confusions like this.
A	Okay can we get on. What's your address Joanne?
S	62, Walford Road.
N	Would you like a cup of tea?
S	Thank you.
	[N goes off up stage]
A	62 Walford, oh I'm not sure.
C	That doesn't sound quite...
A	I don't think so, Walford, it's not road *[C&A whisper]*.
C	What do you do when you're in a car Joanne?
S	Drive?
A	Walford Drive excellent, good work.
C	Thanks.
	Right, where were you last night?
S	I was at home.
A	*[Adjusts her collar as a sign to her colleagues]*
C	*[More aggressively]* What were you doing?
S	I was at home watching the telly.
A	*[In a conciliatory tone]* Surely not all night?
S	Yes.
C	Yeah yeah.
A	*[Adjusts collar]*

C	*[More aggressive]* Yeah yeah.
S	I was.
A	*[Adjusts collar again, more urgently]* and you really didn't go out at all?
S	No!
C	We don't believe you Joanne, where's your alibi, what's your bullshit? Let's hear it!
A	Ease off Brian!
C	I thought you...
A	Were you with anyone who can back you up Joanne?
S	Yes, my flat mate, Shaun.
A	Shaun *[Making a note in the group's spiral bound notebook]*.
C	Shaun is it?
S	Yes.
C	And you were?
S	Shaun and I were at home watching TV together all night.
C	And Shaun will back that up will he?
A	If Shaun were here say and we asked "where were you last night?"
C	"Last night? Yeah we were in watching TV, you know, *The Bill* then that film with John Wayne in it that Joanne likes".
A	For example?
S	Probably.
A	And you're sure about that?
C	You don't want to change your story?
A	Shaun was with you all night?
S	Yes.
A	Well let's ask him shall we? Bring him in!
C	Right.
A	Bet that's a bit of a shock isn't it.
	[C goes off upstage and immediately returns with N who is now wearing a coat]
A	All right Shaun sit down. What's your name?
N	Shaun.
A	Thank you, and your address?
N	It's ur *[surreptitiously reading address from spiral pad]* 62 Walford Drive and I've never seen her before in my entire life! *[Whispering to C]* Is that okay?
A	*[Taps her nose whilst looking at C]*

C	*[Ushers N out]* Come on.
N	I hope I was of some help to you there.
C	No, not really.
S	*[Pointing after N]* That's not Shaun.
A	No, I know. Sorry about that. Where were we?
S	I was watching television.
C	I've seen Shaun out.
A	Thank you.
C	He was very confused.
A	I can imagine. Right watching television at home all last night, that's funny because *[laces her fingers together repeatedly again]* because...
C	...because so did we!
A	No! That's funny because we have a witness who puts you in a restaurant last night.
C	Right! Ring any bells? A restaurant, in Kings Cross?
S	Where?
A	La Fourchette.
C	Who's that Joanne?
A	Like French food do you?
C	Who's dobbed you in?
A	Six courses?
S	I was at home. I had cheese on toast!
A	Ah, Gallois rare morceau.
C	Avec fromage n'est-ce pas?
A	Bien sure bien.
C	"Mais je suis dans ma maison avec Shaun!"
A	You can't have been at home because we have a *[N enters upstage in full chef's outfit]* taxi driver who's willing to swear he took you there. *[N exits]*
S	When?
A	Last night.
S	But I.
A	At 9.30.
C	He'll swear blind.
S	I was watching the TV, with Shaun, eating cheese on toast.
A	Oh really?

S	I don't even like french food!
C	A likely story.
	[They wait for the taxi driver]
A	Where is he? How long since we phoned him? Is this firm reliable?
C	Quarter of an hour. He'll be on his way. He's just pulling up outside... He'll honk his horn... I'll go and get him.
	[C disappears to find N who appears immediately without him]
N	Hello my name's Dave, I'm a cabby.
A	Take a seat. Right Dave, what's your occupation?
N	I'm a cabby. All right love, nice to see you again. Got back all right the other day?
A	You've seen this young woman before?
N	Yeah, I know her all right, I had her in my cab just the other day.
A	The other day?
N	Yes.
C	Yesssst t t er...
N	Yesterday.

A	Really?
C	Really?
N	Yeah.
A	Well that's very interesting isn't it Joanne?
C	That's very interesting.
A	Now then Dave this is very helpful. *[Whispering]* keep it up. If you could think carefully. Where did you pick young Joanne up yesterday?
	[Through the remainder of the taxi driver's evidence A is performing ever more elaborate charades behind S's back to prompt N to give the required answers]
N	Well I picked her up from... from her house and er...
A	Good and what time was this?
N	It must have been about, 9 o'clock, first thing in the morning I'd just taken her to work. At night! What am I saying, 9 o'clock at night. It's dark at both times of the day you just/
A	And where did you take her?
C	*[In N's ear]* It's very important you get this right!
N	I know.
C	Think carefully.
N	Where did I drop her off? At the er dentists in er cafe, a restaurant... at a restaurant!
C	Where was this?
N	In Hat Place, in Hatfield, Hatfield Place, Cross, by in Bishop Finger just by Bishop Finger tube station near the Beefeater Shop, fencing department in Rackhams in the Smashed Fingers at Kings Cross, Kings Cross!
C	Right, thank you very much Dave the taxi driver.
	[C ushers N out]
A	Oh dear Joanne it's not looking very good is it?
C	For the benefit of the tape, the witness is sweating, profusely.
A	What's this?
S	A pen.
A	OK. And this.
S	A fist. A finger. Pen, fist, finger, fist, finger, fist, finger, pen.
A	Where were you last night?
S	At home watching telly!
A	Have you been to Cuba?
S	No!

A	Have you seen me before?
S	No!
A	Good, is that good?
S	Yeah *[adjusts collar]*.
A	Well it probably doesn't matter, whatever. There's probably been some misunderstanding.
C	That's bullshit. She's lying through her teeth and we all know it. Shaun denies ever having met her, a cab driver swears he took her to Kings Cross last night and we all know what that means and who the hell are you?
N	*[N has entered wearing a dress which is too small for him]* Joanne there you are! Where've you been? I've been worried sick. I've been walking round town all afternoon.
A	Would you like a seat?
N	Thank you very much love, my feet are killing me. Why didn't you phone? I've been worried sick.
C	*[Whispering to N]* What are you doing?
A	Would you like a cup of coffee?
N	Tea please, nice and sweet. I couldn't get one in Debenhams, I didn't have any money left. Where were you last night Joanne?
S	I was at home mum.
N	I tried to phone you and there was no answer. I thought something had happened.
S	I'm sorry Mum, we had the TV on, we didn't hear anything.
N	I was worried about you.
S	There's nothing to worry about Mum, I'm fine.
N	I do worry about you Joanne
S	I know you do Mum, but you shouldn't.
N	I can't help it.
S	I can look after myself now Mum.
N	I know. How's the flat?
S	It's good, you should come round.
N	And Shaun?
S	That's good too Mum. You'd like him if you met him.
A	There you go Mrs... Miss?
C	Mrs.
A	There you go Mrs.
N	Thank you love. I do miss him you know.

S   I know Mum, so do I.
N   Have they given you a cup of tea?
S   No.
A   No, she's not allowed a cup of tea.
C   She's on 'no tea' rations.
S   I'm not allowed a cup of tea Mum.
N   Oh Joanne what have you done? I'm in an awful state.
S   Oh Mum, how did you let yourself get like this? Look at you.
N   You're ashamed of me!
S   No, I'm not ashamed mum but please try and look after yourself. It breaks my heart to see you like this.
N   It's you, it's the worry, where were you?
C   Okay that's it, time's up. Come on, I can't stand any more of this. *[Starts a struggle to get N to leave]*
N   You can't make me go!
C   Watch me!
A   Bye Mrs.Watt, nice to meet you.
N   Bye love, bye Joanne, I'll visit again soon.
    [N is bundled out by C]

C	Quite a responsibility ay Joanne?
A	Upset us all that has.
C	Very upsetting that was, very upsetting. She's only going to get worse Jo, have you thought about her in your plans? No one wants to see their mum like that.
S	No, it was quite upsetting.
C	She's probably falling down the stairs as we speak. They're lethal in this place.

[A has been drawing a cartoonish house on the spiral pad, now she shows it to S]

A	Do you recognise this?
S	It's a house.
A	Of course it's a house, whose house is it Joanne?
S	Don't know.
A	Yours, it's your house!
S	It's not.
A	Don't try to deny it.
S	It's not, there's no front door.
A	Oh you're right. Okay hang on, bear with me. *[Draws in a front door]* Right do you recognise this?
S	That's my house!
A	Exactly! 62 Walford Drive, 9.30 last night, so where are you?
S	I'm at the window.
A	No you're, oh.
C	Yeah, there she is in the window.
A	No, no, that's supposed to be Shaun, it's too tall for you.
S	It's not Shaun. Shaun's got dark curly hair.
A	Oh, I'm rubbish at this!
S	Well it's easy, you've put the front door in so just draw some curtains in to cover me up or something.
A	Will, will that work?
S	If you do it neatly no one will know.
A	I will.
S	You'll have to forget.
A	What's that?
S	It's like this but later.
A	I see.

The Plumber Philosopher

N	And what about you? *[The interrogation turns onto C]*
C	Me?
N	What's your place in the grand scheme of things?
C	I'm...
N	Are you Joanne's brother?
C	Yes.
N	And do you know why you're here?
C	To...
N	To answer some questions, some quite important questions this is my colleague...
S	Jo. Name?
C	John.
N	John Watt?
C	No, Kennedy.
A	What, not Watt?
C	No, Kennedy.
S	Not the John Kennedy?
C	No.
S	Initial?
C	F.
N	Address?
C	Reservoir Road, number three, top of the hill, can't miss it, massive white frontage.
N	All right Bill, what do you do?
C	I'm a plumber.
S	Plumber?
N	A plumber is it? And you expect us to believe that?
C	I am a plumber.
N	Get up scum bag!
S	What!
N	Come on, stand up shit face. In that chair, sit. *[It's the same chair]* Right Mr. President. Now, let's get down to brass tacks shall we?
A	For the benefit of the tape, Mr. Kennedy is combing his hair. *[He's not]*
N	Why are we all here Jack, hum?
C	You wanted me to...
N	What's the point of it all pretty boy?

C What?
N What's it all for?
C What? What's what for?
N It.
C It?
N It.
C What?
S It!
A It!
N It!
C It? What sex!
N No!
C It's for when two people who love each other dearly and – shouldn't your parents have told you?
N No. It. Life. Us. The human race. Why were we put on the Earth arsehole?
C What!
N We can't get born then work ourselves to death for no reason. There's got to be something else, what is it?
C I don't know!
N Come on Shit Bird, think!
A What are we here for Bobby? That's all he's asking.
S Come on John.
N Why are we all here?
C I don't know. I'm just a plumber. I don't know.
A Are you happy with that John?
C With what?
A Fixing pipes.
C It's all right.
A Is that all you aspire to?
S You see that doesn't add up to us John.
A But does it give you fulfilment?
C Some.
N But not much.
C No.
N So what's it all for Jizz Freak?
C What?
N Get up.
C Why should I?

N	Come on stand up, stand up! Sit in that chair! *[Different chair]* Right then Big J, let's get down to brass tacks shall we? Why are we all here K Boy, hum?
C	I honestly don't know. I haven't done anything.
S	That's not the point.
C	I'm a plumber.
N	That's not the point either, Mr. President.
A	The point is Frank, what's the purpose of existence?
S	Take your time.
A	For the tape, Mr. Kennedy is fumbling with a packet of cigarettes. *[He's not]*
C	I've not given it much thought really.
N	So think about it now, the reason for being.
S	Come on Johnny.
C	I don't think anyone knows do they?
A	You know Johnny.
S	Don't hold out on us.
C	No really I don't.
A	Why are we all here?
C	Um.
N	Come on big boy.
S	Say something.
A	Spill it.
C	Um, we're here to uh...
N	Come on, what is it?
A	Give it up.
C	I can't think.
N	What is it?
C	I don't know! To have a good time?
N	WHAT?
C	To have a good time.
A	"To have a good time" is that it?
N	Is that it? Is that your answer?
C	Well I suppose so?
S	*[Writing in the pad]* "To have a good time"
N	What do you mean 'to have a good time'?
C	What do you think I mean? *[Turning the interrogation]*
N	Well it's your good time.
C	I don't think you know what a good time is.

N	I do.
C	I don't think you do.
N	I do.
C	So what is it?
N	Well, it's making friends isn't it.
C	That's it and have you got a lot of friends?
N	Yeah, I've got a few.
C	What are their names?
N	I don't think I want to...
S	Names.
N	They aren't in trouble are they?
S	Names!
N	Heather.
S&C	And?
N	Mark
C	And?
S	So it's all about making friends with Heather and Mark, is that it? Is that what it's all about?
A	And that's the true essence of existence is it?
S	We're all here to make friends with Heather and Mark.
N	Ah well yeah, I suppose.
C	We don't even know Heather and Mark. Where does that leave us?
N	Well...
C	Does that make our lives meaningless?
N	Well no, you've got your own/
C	What are we here for then?
A	We don't know who Heather and Mark are.
N	Well you've got your own friends I guess.
A	Will you introduce us?
C	How do you know?
N	I was just using Heather and Mark as an example, I don't mean they're the only people you should know.
C	Don't wriggle out of it. Sit in that chair come on.
	[To N] Stand up. Sit in this chair. *[3]*
S	*[To A]* sit in that chair. *[1]*
A	*[To S]* Get up.
S	*[To N]* Stand up. Sit in that chair. *[2]*
A	*[To C]* You, sit down. [3]

N	*[To A]* On your feet
C	*[To S]* You, sit here. *[2]*
A	*[To N]* You, sit there. *[1]*
S	*[To A]* You, in that chair. *[1]*
A	*[To N]* Get up.
N	*[To C]* Back off.
C	*[To N]* Park it .
A	(To S) Right, get up.
N	*[To A]* On your feet.
C	*[To S]* Back off.
A	*[To C]* Shut it.
S	*[To N]* Stand up.
N	*[To A]* You, in that chair. *[2]*
A	*[To S]* You, in that chair. *[3]*
S	*[To A]* Zip it.
N	*[To S]* Leave it.
A	*[To N&S]* Cool it.
S	*[To N]* Stand up.
C	*[To N]* Sit down.
S	*[To N]* Stand up.
A	*[To S]* Leave him where he is!
	So Heather and Mark hold the key to existence do they?
N	Well no.
A	Can you get hold of them?
N	I barely know them.
A	I think we should get them in here, this Heather and Mark.
N	They'll be at work, they'll both be at work.
A	What do they do Heather and Mark?
C	Super Beings is it?
N	No, er Heather's a secretary and Mark is an engineer.
S	*[Writing]* Engineer.
A	Okay we're pulling them in; addresses *[she pushes notepad to N to write on]*
N	I don't think they'd be able to help much.
S	So, what's the main reason for being on this Earth... *[checks name in notes then addressing A]* Joanne? Now he's said his friends Heather and Mark but that wasn't all together convincing.

N	What are you saying?
C	I've met them, trust me, they're gobshites.
N	Look, I don't appreciate that!
C	They're gobshites, what's your problem?
S	So now, now we're going to try a different tack, okay?
A	Okay.
S	I'm going to give some options and you choose the one that you think is correct.
A	Okay.
S	So Joanne, what's the main reason for us being on the Earth? Is it to: A – Come to the park. B – Do God's will. *[A awaits a third option]* What's your answer? A or B?
A	Um...
S	A or B?
A	B.
S	Do Gods will?
N	And you're sure?
A	Can you say the question again please?
S	What's the main reason for us being on the Earth, is it: A – To come to the park, B – To do God's will.
A	B – To do God's will.
C	*[Writing]* To do God's will. Do you believe in God?
S	Is there a God?
A	Er no.
C	You don't believe in God but you believe/
N	in doing God's will.
A	I mean, well it's a better answer isn't it. I mean, it's a better answer than/
N	It's not a better answer if you don't believe in God Billy.
S	Do you believe in the park Billy?
A	Well the... I believe there is a park.
S	Do you believe there is a God?
A	Well I don't umm, I don't practice a religion or/
S	Well you don't have to be religious to believe in the park do you Brian?
N	Are you saying to us that the purpose of existence is to go to

	the park?
C	With Heather and Mark?
A	No, because because I said B – Do God's will.
N	But you don't believe in God, so you must mean A – Go to the park.
A	That's not fair!
N	Life's not fair Joanne.
C	The sooner you learn that the better.
N	We can't just go to the park whenever we want to.
C	Some of us have to work.
N	We can't all swig cider in the park all day waiting.
C	Waiting for Heather and Mark to appear.
N	Waiting for Heather and Mark to appear and the world to end.
S	For the benefit of the tape the witness is combing her hair *[She's not]*.
C	I don't believe you've fully got the hang of these multiple choice questions Senator, so I'll give you one that's slightly easier okay. What day of the week is it today, is it: A – Monday, B: – Tuesday C – Wednesday
A:	Well it's/
C	*[Holds his hand up to halt her]* D – Thursday, E – Friday, F – Saturday, G – Sunday or H – None of the above?
A	What do I get if I get it right?
C	You get a prize.
A	C – Wednesday.
N	Wrong, you're wrong!
C	Unlucky it was a lovely prize wasn't it, Carriage Clock
N	It was a lovely prize, Carriage Clock.
A	Look I don't understand. Why are we here?
C	Sorry, what was the question?
A	Why are we all here?
N	What are the options?
A	Don't ask me.
C	*[Turning to S]* Joanne?
N	For the benefit of the tape the witness is conferring with her lawyer. *[She's not]*
	Do you understand the question Joanne?
S	No, not really.

C	You never think about it yourself? You don't ever think? You don't ever get up on a dark winter's morning, another early morning call to fix another leaky radiator... you don't ever think, "there's got to be more to life than this"?
S	Well, sometimes.
N	So you understand the question, now what's the answer?
C	Does it give meaning to your life Joanne, fixing those leaky pipes, helping out the old folk?
S	Well, some meaning, some.
C	Making sure the system's fixed. The system in someone's bathroom is the same as the system we live in. One little system effecting a much much bigger system. Holding tanks, dripping taps, dodgy flushes, everything about to go down the pan.
S	Well I don't know about that.
C	Believe in it Jack, run with it, how it all links together. You're there fixing this leaking system of ours Jackie, unblocking the waste pipes, securing the guttering, keeping us all warm at nights.
S	Well if you like yeah, yeah.
	Do you have a mate Bobby?
C	My name's John.
N	Answer the question John.
S	Do you have a mate Bobby?
C	My name's/
N	Answer the question John.
C	Do I have a mate?
N	That's just repeating the question.
C	Yes, plenty, thank you very much.
A	I think they mean, do you have a plumbers mate, someone to hand you the spanners, that kind of thing.
C	Yeah, Dave.
S	Dave is it?
C	Yeah.
S	And you can vouch for him?
C	He's not in trouble is he? That's not what/
S	Say, for instance, Dave goes home at nights, you say:
N	"Night Dave, have a good one"
A	"Cheers John, see you in the morning"

N	"Yep see you"
S	How do you actually know he goes home?
N	*[Turning himself into the suspect]* Well he lives in Hall Green.
S	How do you know?
N	Well I've seen his house.
C	And have you been to his house?
N	A couple of times.
A	But have you seen him at his house when you're not there?
N	Well no, of course not.
S	So where is he then? Do you see what I mean?
N	Not really, you'll have to ask his girlfriend.
A	He's got a girlfriend has he?
N	Yeah, Cheryl.
S	Do you need Dave, Bobby?
C	Well, he's OK, not so good at the soldering but he makes a good cup of/
S	That's not what I mean is it? I mean, do you <u>need</u> him?
C	Yes, he's helpful.
N	And your wife Bobby, she goes to work?
A	"That's me off Bobby"
N	"OK sweet heart, see you later?"
A	"What time?"
N	"Six, unless Dave doesn't show again" *[They get sucked into an overextended improvisation of banal domestic arrangements being made]*
N	Anyway you get the idea. She goes to work but how do you know she's really there?
C	Well she gets paid.
N	But that's not really evidence is it?
C	If she's not there why would she get paid?
N	Because um…
A	Because… it might suit the bank manager to … keep things ticking over.
S	Does this so called money validate your wife's existence?
C	No.
N	Exactly! So *[holds the teapot under the table]* how do you know this teapot exists?
C	When?
N&A	Now.

C	Well it's under the table isn't it.
N&A	Is it?
C	Well you're holding it there.
N	But am I? But am I?
C	*[To C & A]* He, is he crackers then?
N	Where is – does the teapot exist?
C	Well it's got tea in it hasn't it?
A	But does it?
N	It does, but how do you know?
C	I heard it sloshing around.
A	Have you tasted any tea?
C	I haven't had any tea, you said there was going to be tea, but I haven't seen any tea yet.
A	You can't see a tea pot so does a tea pot exist?
	[N has put the teapot on the table]
C	Yes.
A	How do you know?
C	Because it's there.
A	Well there's one there now yeah, but when it was under the table did it exist?
C	Well it was under the table then wasn't it.
A	*[To N]* It would be more helpful if it was under the table.
	[N holds the teapot under the table]
A	Does the teapot exist?
C	Yes.
A	How do you know?
N	How can you tell?
C	I can see it under the table.
	[N puts the teapot up under his shirt, it is hot]
A	Now, does it exist?
C	*[Playing along]* I don't know I can't see it.
A	Exactly! That's our point.
C	What's your point?
A	How do you know it exists?
C	Well I don't, I can't see it.
N	Absolutely!
C	But it's under his shirt.
A	How do you know it's there?
C	I saw him put it there.

A   Good point.
N   But if you hadn't see me put it under there how would you know John?
C   My name's Bobby.
S   Answer the question Bobby.
C   Look if it wasn't under his jumper you wouldn't be asking me these bloody stupid questions then would you?
A   Also a very good point. If a tree falls over in a forest/
C   Does anyone scream?
A   Right, I've obviously asked that one before. What did you say that time?
C   When?
A   When I asked you that question first time round.
C   You haven't asked me that question.
A   If a tree falls over in the forest/
N   How do we know it's made a sound?
C   Depends what it lands on.
A   If it lands on some... some crackling bracken.
C   It probably would.
S   Probably would.
A&N   Yeah it probably would wouldn't it.
A   Great, good.
N   *[With notepad and pen]* Shall I put probably?
A   What are the options?
S   *[Frustrated]* Just put 'yes'.
N   Great.

Word association (with holiday)

C   Tea?
A   Coffee.
C   Coffee?
N   Please.
C   Coffee?
S   Thanks.
C   Okay. *[Exits]*
A   Right Joanne, thanks for that, you've been very helpful so far. Now if you'd like to come back over here, we're going to ask you some more questions.
N   Actually they're not really questions.

A	No, we're going to say a few words.
N	But there's no pressure.
A	No, we just want you to/
N	Actually there is some pressure.
A	Well yes, of course, we want you to concentrate hard.
N	We want you to think, no we don't.
A	Not at all.
N	You've got to be spontaneous. We're going to say some words.
A	Any words.
N	Random words.
A	But they won't be.
N	No, because they're all carefully planned.
A	There's a careful logic for what we are about to say.
N	And after we've said our word we want you to say the first word that comes into your head.
A	Straight afterwards.
N	Absolutely immediately.
S	Could we start?
A	Could we?
C	Sure.
A	You understand?
S	Yes.
A	Okay we'll start.
N	We'll kick off. Which way round are we going?
A	I think we just say a word and she responds.
N	Oh right. *[Tries to think of a word]*
A	Do you want me to say a word?
N	Yeah. *[A sits in his chair and tries to think of a word]*
A	That's more difficult than you'd think.
	[Whispering with N] We can't say that!
N	Why not?
A	It's a leading question.
N	Isn't that the whole point?
A	What?
N	That they're leading questions.
A	No they're supposed to be 'open for interpretation'.
N	Won't that be confusing?
A	You're right, what about *[whispers]*?

N   We can't say that.
A   Why not?
N   It's pornographic.
A   It's not it's 'psychological'.
N   What about. *[Whisper]*
A   That's worse.
N   Is it?
A   *[Whisper]*
N   Oh you're right!
S   Cheese.
C   Bacon.
S   Water.
C   Swimming.
S   Violin.
C   Mozart.
S   Timpani.
C   Lighthouse.
S   Draughts.
C   Chess.
S   Cheese.
C   Bacon.
S   German.
C   Forest.
S   French.
C   Cheese.
S   Bacon.
C   Sandwich.
S   Golf.
C   Cricket.
S   Tea.
C   Sandwich.

[During the word association]
N   What?
A   Hold on!
    Wait, hold on.
N   That's our job.
    It's impressive.
S   Golf.

C	Cricket.
S	Hockey.
C	Sticks.
S	Fire.
A	Forest.
S	Fields.
C	Grass.
A	Crickets.
C	Golf.
S	Carts.
C	Cars.
A	Motorway.
C	Bridges.
S	Rivers.
C	Countryside.
A	Grass.
N	Ah, one of those electric lawn mower things, you know they're orange and/
A	Idiot!
C	Terry.
A	No!
C	Yes!
A	Shhhh.
C	Woosh!
A	Brian.
C	Me *[A hits C]* ouch!
A	*[To S]* Sorry about that. You're getting the idea?
S	Why are we doing this?
N	We're doing this to get inside your mind.
A	To bypass your natural censors and inhibitions.
S	Right.
C	Left.
N	To get to the real you.
C	Me.
N	Stop it.
C	Sorry, I've stopped.
N	Thank you.
C	Pleasure.
A	Brian!

C	Me. I'll, I'll stand over here, out of the way.
	[C sits on chair upstage]
A	Right we're going to bypass all your natural censors and inhibitions and discover the real you. Are you ready?
S	Yes.
A	Now you find may this a chastening and a degrading experience.
S	Right.
N	You may find yourself in tears by the end, you know, having revealed your very soul, your basest, most deeply concealed animal instincts.
S	Okay.
A	We may reveal within you the repressed drives of, of a fascist dictator.
N	For example.
A	The paedophilic leanings of a deranged pervert barely on the cusp of humanity.
S	Right.
N	Okay, the first word that enters your head, right?
S	Left.
N	No, we haven't started yet.
S	Okay.
N	Now.
S	Then.
N	No, we still haven't started. Tell you what, I'll say the word then nod, then you answer, okay?
S	Right.
N	Okay, prepare to lay yourself bare before us. Cheese *[nods]*.
S	Bacon.
N	Sandwich. *[Nods]*
S	Golf.
N	Cricket. *[Nods]*
S	Grass.
N	Flymo. *[Nods]*
S	Electricity.
N	Death. Tell you what, could you manage without the nodding, it's beginning to really...
S	Sure.
N	Thanks. Right where were we?

C	*[Referring to his notes on the pad]* Death.
N	Wow, we're getting somewhere, what did she say before that?
C	She didn't.
S	You said Death.
N	Did I? When did I say that?
C	Just after she said electricity.
N	Why did I say that?
A	I don't know.
N	That's worrying, isn't it?
C	I don't know.
N	Should I be worried? That's natural isn't it Electricity, Death, what else could you say?
C	Light bulb.
A	Fuses.
	[C & A Improvise a long list of electricity related words]
S	Love.
CAN	Love?
S	You know, the electricity between two people.
N	Oh, can she have that? Love.
C	Yes.
A	I suppose so.
N	Okay. Love.
S	You.
N	Me?
S	Love.
N	You.
S	Love.
N	Me.
S	Yes. Love.
N	Terror.
S	Affection.
N	Distress.
S	Compliance.
N	Compliance? What/
C	Doing what you're told.
N	Oh, safety.
S	Embrace.
N	Hug.

N   Okay, Mother.
S   Mother.
N   That's what I just said.
S   Mother.
N   Right, school.
S   School.
N   Work.
S   Holiday.
N   The sea.
S   Weekend.
N   Grass.
S   Work.

N	Nothing.
S	Money.
N	Nothing.
S	Love.
N	Nothing.
S	Dancing.
N	Nothing.
S	Dreaming.
N	Nothing.
S	Freedom.
N	Nothing.
S	Aspiration.
N	Nothing.
S	Sweetness.
N	Nothing.
S	Tears.
N	Nothing.
S	Singing.
N	Nothing.
S	Poetry.
N	Nothing.
S	Running.
N	Nothing.
C	Terry.
S	Laughing.
N	Nothing.
C	Terry.
S	Your colleagues.
C	Terry.
N	Nothing.
S	Embrace.
N	Nothing.
	Something.
	Dancing.
	Swaying.
	Cranes.
	Mast.
	Church.
	Tower.

	Blocks.
	Rubble.
	Dust.
	Footprints.
	Stairs.
	Attic.
	Window.
C	Sky.
A	Stars.
S	Navigation.
A	Lights.
C	Vapour.
S	Trails.
A	Planes.
C	Holiday.
A	Yeah.
C	Flying.
S	West.
N	Yeah.
C	Over the sea.
N	We're on the way.
A	Yeah.
S	Flying into the sunset.
A	That's us.
C	We're going on holiday.
N	Suitcase.
C	Bucket.
S	Spade.
A	Yeah.
C	A lovely holiday in the Caribbean. Wouldn't it be lovely, being able to dip our toes in the ocean, feel the warm sand beneath you. Going to the bar for a delicious cocktail. Then perhaps a shower, get changed and/
S	Play a little snooker.
C	Yeah! Pot Black then off to the restaurant, order a beautiful meal.
N	Lighthouse blinking far out to sea.
A	Lovely yeah.
S	Cowboy movie on the telly.

N	Soft music.
A	Gentle surf.
C	Sun setting like an orange... like an orange.
S	Setting.
C	Yeah.
N	Yeah.
A	Yeah, Bacardi.
S	TV on the beach.
A	*The Bill*.
S	Yeah.
C	Lovely.
N	That's it.
S	Beautiful.
C	Easy.
A	Or maybe it's Vienna.
N	Berlin.
A	A foggy night, trilby hat, trench coat. It's cold, you're leaning up against a wall.
N	Checkpoint Charlie.
S	I preferred the Caribbean.
A	Waiting for him to walk out. You know he's out there.
N	Yeah.
A	Deep in the night.
S	I liked the beach.
N	Yeah.
A	You've got to find him.
N	Sure.
A	This is what you've been waiting for.
N	Sure.
A	The day of reckoning.
C	You know that he knows that you know he's out there, somewhere.
N	Big Bill Werbeniuk.
C	Harry Lime.
A	Orson Wells.
S	Pina Colada.
C	There's a rattle at the door.
S	The handle turns.
N	"Who's there?"

A	A man enters. *[C is acting as this man]*
S	And?
A	He takes two paces, then stops.
S	And?
A	He looks around the room.
S	And?
A	And says...
S	What?
C	"It's Big Bill, I've come to repossess your furniture"
N	He wouldn't say that!
A	He did, we've got it on tape.
N	That's not Bill's style.
A	How do you know?
N	He's a mate.
C	"It's Big Bill, I've come to repossess your furniture."
A	Just like that.
N	I can't believe it!
A	Believe in it Jackie.
S	What's this? *[Holding up a mug]*
N	A mug.
A	Who am I?
N	A mug.
C	Who's this? *[Shows N stick figure drawing of a woman]*
N	I've never seen her before in my life!
S	Dust.
N	Ashes.
S	Money.
N	Paper.
S	Clouds.
N	Maps.
S	Footprints.
N	Beach.
S	Beach.
N	Snooker.
C	Snooker.
N	Lighthouse.
A	Lighthouse.
C	Spandau.
N	Ballet.

C	Some day.
N	Soon.
A	Heaven.
N	Is a place on Earth.
C	Europe.
N	*The Final Count Down.*
A	The Beat.
N	*Mirror in the Bathroom.*
C	Madness.
N	*Return of the Los Palmas 7.*
C	The Birmingham Six.
N	Flat back four.
C	UB40.
N	New Deal.
C	New Order.
N	Blue Monday.
C	Mondays.
N	Don't like 'em.
C	Tuesday.
N	Good bye Ruby.
C	Wednesday.
A	Terry.
N	Hall.
S	Friday.
N	Fish.
S	Catholic.
N	Confession.
S	Guilt.
N	Satin.
S	The Moon.
N	Moonies.
S	School.
N	Moonies.
S	Authority.
N	Moonies!
S	The Queen.
N	Moonies!
S	Back seat of the bus!
N	Moonies!

A	Terry.
N	Hall.
C	The Guilford Four.
N	The Fun Boy Three.
C	*The Tunnel of Love.*
N	Channel Tunnel.
C	Friday Night.
N	Saturday Morning.
C	Ley lines.
N	Hippies.
C	White lines.
N	Yellow lines.
C	Sweet temptation.
N	Temptations.
C	The Specials.
N	The Police.
A	Terry.
N	Hall.
C	Terry are you one of The Specials?
N	How did you find out?
S	Your so called 'friends'.
C	"No thank's, I've just had one." "No, whatever, I'll call you in a bit, yeah, later. Keep it safe" "Maybe, I don't know she said she wasn't bothered but I fancy one" Sound familiar?
N	No!
S	Okay how about this. "Na, I can't be arsed really"
A	"Oh come on, it'll be fun"
S	"Huh?"
A	"It will"
S	"You reckon?"
A	"It was last time"
S	"You think so?"
A	"Oh come on"
S	"Will Mark be there?"
A	"Of course he'll be there, it's Heather's party"
S	"No, not Heather's Mark. Tall Mark, you know"

A	"With the glasses?"
S	"What, Sue's ex-Mark?"
A	"Yes, stuttering Mark with the sun tan?"
S	"Yes"
A	"Oh he'll be there!"
S	"Great I'll come!"
A	What about that?
N	What about it?
S	Do you recognise it?
N	No, is it from a film?
S	Don't deny it.
N	Deny what?
A	It's you isn't it. I'm you! We've had your bugged for months.
N	Who said you could do that?
C	We don't need permission Shaun.
S	What was that all about then Mr.President, that little charade?
N	I suppose I didn't want to go out.
A	No, I was you.
N	Oh, then I did want to go out.
C	And why did you want to go out?
N	Maybe I'm claustrophobic.
C	And what's that mean?
S	What does it feel like?
N	It means I don't like confined spaces.
S	But what does it feel like?
N	Claustrophobic.
S	I know what you say it is, but what does it feel like?
N	I don't know.
S	I thought you were claustrophobic.
N	I am!
S	So what does it feel like?
N	Tense.
S	What do you mean?
N	Claustrophobic, tense!
S	Yes but what does that feel like?
N	It feels hot, sweaty.
S	And what does that feel like?
N	Like this. *[He takes her hand and puts it under his arm pit]*

	Do you get the feeling?
S	I think so.
N	Do you want to know anything else?
S	Um, no. This will do for now, I think, thank you.
N	It's claustrophobic being a hero.
S	Is that what you are?
N	Yes.
S	Am I?
	[S offers her arm pit, N feels it]
N	No.
S	Oh.
C	*[Feeling his own arm pit]* I'm not, pity.
A	*[Feeling her own arm pit]* I think I might be!
C	Well done!
N	*[With notebook]* Is that a definite 'yes' then Wendy?
A	Yeah.
N	Great. *[Writing]* Wendy and of course, me.
N	Are we allowed to smoke in here?
A	No.
C	No, it's a fire hazard. You don't smoke anyway.
N	No.
S	That's good because you shouldn't smoke.
N	No, I don't.
S	That's good.
A	It's bad for your chest.
S	It's bad for you.
C	Bronchitis.
A	Bronchitis?
S	You should make a law against it. I mean they aught to sort out what they make laws for and and what they don't make laws for. I mean, they have all these law enforcements for things which are ridiculous like, you can't walk in the grass in the park and you can't phone people after a certain time of night and you have to give up your seat on the bus. They should make a law about smoking.
CAN	Yeah.

Hostage

N	What do you think you're doing?
S	Lazing around?
A	You've been no use at all.
N	We haven't got time to deal with people like you.
C	I was thinking.
S	Don't think, speak.
A	Time is money.
S	Name?
C	Billy.
A	Billy what?
C	Billy Holiday.
N	What's your job Billy Holiday?
C	I'm a plumber.
N	That's not what you told us last week.
C	Last week?
N	Tuesday, Interview Room 4.
A	We've got the tapes.
N	Said you were a hot shot.
C	Who did?
S	You did.
N	You were drunk.
A	Your Mum was disappointed in you.
N	She was in tears.
C	She's always been very proud of me.
A	Not now.
N	Not after what we told her.
C	What did you tell her?
A	Never you mind.
N	We had her in here.
A	She said you were 'something' in the city.
C	I am, I'm a plumber. I work in the city.
N	Plumber with interests is it?
A	How much are you worth Billy?
S	Twenty grand?
C	I don't know.
S	Fifty grand?
C	It depends where you live.
S	Sixty grand?

A	Where do you live Billy?
C	Highgate.
S	Two hundred grand?
C	Yes.
N	Two hundred grand, for a plumber, that's not right!
C	I've got interests..
N	What are your interests?
A	Are you a player?
C	Computers.
N	You play with computers?
S	Are you a wiz kid or a geek?
A	A hacker or a/
C	What's that?
A	Do you hack into defence systems?
C	Yes.
A	And bank accounts?
C	Yes.
N	Do you succeed, Geek?
C	Yes, last night I got into your account.
N	What?
C	You're in a bit of debt aren't you?
N	Well.
C	You've got a lot of debt.
N	Well...
C	More now than before I got in.
N	What?
C	I added a couple of noughts to your overdraft.
N	I don't believe it! Why did you do that?
C	I thought it'd be a laugh.
N	A laugh!
A	Are you in debt Darren?
N	Well a bit but/
A	You should sort that out.
S	You shouldn't live beyond your means.
N	Hold on!
S	What if we all did that, where would we be then?
A	An artificial boom, fuelled by consumer credit, is that what you want Darren?
N	No.

A	And all its attendant inflationary pressures. Do you want those Darren?
N	No.
S	So who's actually earning the money?
A	It's all about wealth generation Darren.
S	Isn't making things the only morally justifiable way of earning a living?
N	Pardon?
C	This job can't pay much.
A	But then you're not contributing much, are you Darren?
N	I do as much as I can, as much as you.
A	But do you get paid as much?
N	I don't know. How much do you get?
A	£19 per hour.
N	What!
S	Really? I'm on £15.
N	What!
A	We'll I've got the extra responsibility.
N	Hold on I'm on £5.50!
A	Yeah but mine's the high risk position.
S	High risk! It's me who's sitting next to him.
A	People get paid what they're worth Darren.
C	You should be more frugal.
N	What do you mean?
C	You should cut down on the luxuries.
A	And the fats.
C	You're porking out a bit.
A	That's not what I was saying.
C	But he is.
A	I think he's nice like that.
N	Like what?
A	A bit porky.
N	I'm not porky, am I porky?
S	No, he's not porky.
A	So what's your idea of porky?
S	It's not about weight is it?
N	It's about how people carry themselves.
S	Exactly!
A	But do you think he's attractive like that?

S	Well...
A	What do you reckon?
C	Don't ask me?
A	Why not?
C	I haven't got an opinion on that.
A	Well get one.
C	Well no, I don't find him attractive.
A	I didn't ask that.
S	She asked if he <u>was</u> attractive.
C	And I said he's not attractive to me.
N	Thank you very much.
C	No problem.
S	She wasn't asking for your subjective opinion. You've got to be objective.
A	If he was a woman would you find him attractive?
C	No.
A&S	Why not?
C	Because he's porky.
S	You are so shallow!
A	You've got no idea about his personality.
S	Or his job prospects.
C	He's in debt.
N	Well that's not my fault.
C	It is, you should be more frugal.
N	I am frugal!
C	Where do you do your shopping?
N	The supermarket, same as you.
C	Well you shouldn't do that.
N	Why not? You do.
C	I get paid more than you, you should go to the market.
N	Why should I... hold on can we get back to the...
S	Overdraft?
N	Hacking into my account *[looks round at the others]*
C	I can't use a computer.
S	Nothing to do with me, I'm strictly vegetarian.
A	I'm a drummer. Keep it live!
C	A drummer, what's the use of that?
A	I don't know, lots of things.
N	Like?

A	I can play the drums.
N	And?
A	And I can get you in.
C	Where?
S	Backstage at The Jug?
A	No, the guest list at...the CBSO... tonight.
C	You're playing at the CBSO tonight?
A	That's it, I'm the soloist, we're doing The Mozart. The violin concerto.
C	Fantastic!
S	Hold on, there aren't any drums in the Mozart violin concerto.
C	There is, there's the timpani.
N	He's right.
A	Anyway, tonight I'm the violinist, it's Shaun on the timpani, he's very good actually.
N	This Shaun...
A	Yeah?
N	What's he look like?
A	Well, he's got curly hair.
N	Hold on give me that pen. *[With quiet prompting from A he draws an artists impression of Shaun. Meanwhile C&S talk to each other]*
C	Do you like music?
S	Yeah, couldn't be without it.
C	Do you fancy coming to a concert tonight?
S	That would be great, what's on?
C	It's The Mozart, it's lovely I can get free tickets.
S	Really?
C	Yeah, I know the drummer. Sorry we haven't been introduced, what's your name?
S	Joanne.
C	Nice name, name of my first kid.
S	You've got children?
C	Just a few.
S	That's nice.
C	Yeah, they're with my ex-wife now.
S	Really?

C	Yeah, a shame really.
S	Where are they?
C	Barbados.
S	Nice.
C	Yeah but I miss them.
S	Why?
C	Because, because they used to be here.
S	Oh.
C	Do you understand?
S	No, not really.
C	Sorry, I shouldn't be going on about it.
S	No, I asked.
C	Do you mind if I ask you something?
S	No, go ahead.
C	You're sure you don't mind?
S	No of course not.
C	What are you worth?
S	I'm sorry, what do you mean?
C	I mean, what's your life worth Joanne?
S	I don't think I understand.
C	What part of the question don't you understand? Well? Okay, so what's the answer?
S	Is this a joke?
C	Do we look like we're joking?
S	No, I suppose not.
C	So what is it?
S	What?
N	Are you deaf?
S	No.
N	So answer the question.
C	What is it Joanne?
A	£100?
S	No.
A	More or less?
S	More, much more!
A	£1000?
S	More. Why do you want to know?
C	Is your life insured?
S	I don't know.

A	How much would you get if you lost an arm?
S	How would you lose an arm?
N	Okay a leg?
S	Look I don't know!
C	How much is your little finger worth, if we delivered it, mail-order, to your Dad?
S	What?
C	Let's put it another way. Would you sacrifice your life for our lives?
S	I don't really know you.
A	Are you worth as much as your principles?
S	What principles?
N	Are you worth as much as Pele?
S	Look, I can't play football if that's what you're asking!
N	Do we look like we're interested in football?
	[Pause]
A	Well do we?
S	No.
CAN	Good.
C	Right I'm going to get a cup of tea, would you like one?
S	Yes please.
C	And you? *[Brushes imaginary fluff from his shoulder]*
N	Yes.
C	And you? *[Repeats action]*
A	Yes.
C	*[Leaves]*
N	Sit in that chair. *[Changes mind about the chair]* Sit in that chair.
	Are you an over or under achiever?
A	Are you a bull or a bear? A man or a mouse? A cat or a fiddle? A pig or a poke? Come on.
	Are you a – a housewife b – a housekeeper or c – homeless I'm sorry I don't think I'm very good at this.
N	You are, you're fine. She's a tough nut. You might have to rough her up a bit.
A	What?
N	You know, put her under pressure, slap her around.
A	Will that help?

S   Probably.
A   How?
N   Try it.
S   Come on.
N   Give it a swing, back of the hand, nice swing, follow through, transfer of weight, ball heel toe, keep it relaxed, nice and natural.
A   I can't!
S   I can take everything you've got!
A   This isn't right!
S   Come on, you'll never beat it out of me you commie bastards! *[Despite not being hit she flies from her chair]* Aaaah!
N   Well done, excellent.
A   I didn't touch her.
C   *[Enters with a mug of tea]* What's, what's been going on here?
N   She was getting gobby, Wendy took exception, the usual you

	know.
A	I didn't touch her!
N	Don't be modest.
C	This is terrible. I strictly told you to ease off.
N	It was beautiful, you should have seen it!
A	I didn't touch her.
C	Then why's she on the floor?
A	I don't know, I didn't touch her.
C	You can't just hit people like that.
N	She was asking for it.
C	I told you to ease off and what do you do?
A	When did you say that?
C	Just before I went to get the tea.
A	You didn't say anything.
C	What do you think this is? *[Brushes imaginary fluff from his shoulder]*
A	What?
C	This. *[Repeats action]*
N	That's 'sod the book, wade into her'.
C	No, it's 'ease off'. That's why I offered her the tea. Would I offer her tea if I wanted you to wade into her?
N	I thought you were being the nice guy.
C	I am the nice guy.
A	I thought this *[adjusting tie]* was 'ease off'.
C	No that means 'go in hard'.
A	Oh shit, that's why earlier you were...
C	Yes, you were doing that, *[adjusting tie]* I was going in hard
N	I saw the tie thing I thought that meant "leave this to me".
C	Oh that's great.
A	Actually mostly I'm just a bit hot when I do this.
N	So what's 'just give me two minutes alone with her'?
A	We haven't got one for that have we?
C	This would do wouldn't it. *[Gesture]*
A	Yeah it's that then.
N	No we discounted that because it looks stupid.
A	How about this? *[Gesture]*
C	Now you're being too literal.
A	What if you do it faster?
C	That's literal and stupid.

N	Fuck it we won't do it then, we'll just say it.
C	We'll say what?
N	"Give me two minutes alone with her".
C	Why do you want that?
N	Well as a tactic.
C	I know about you, you two, and your 'tactics'.
A	What?
C	I've seen you. It's so obvious. I've seen you in Tesco cruising the aisles. Ready washed salads, Hollandaise sauce, don't try and deny it. I've seen you at the delicatessen counter with your number eyeing up the hummus. I've seen you with your baguettes, lingering over the wine offers. You and your flexi-time at the freshly baked cakes, counting the calories. I've seen you with your bottled beers. Don't try and deny it! Eco toilet roll neatly packed arguing about what gin to buy. I fucking hate you. I do. I fucking do. *[Sees S on the floor again]* Shit. Are you all right?
S	I'm fine.
C	Come on love wake up.
S	I am awake.
C	Wake up. My name's John, what's your name?
S	Joanne.
C	Great that's it, where do you live Joanne?
S	Near here.
C	And is it nice there? Keep looking at me.
S	Yes.
C	*[To A]* Will you get her something!
N	Like what?
C	I don't know, a brandy.
A	Would a cup of tea do?
N	I'm sure that would be fine – plenty of sugar. *[A exit]*
C	What's my name?
S	John.
C	Do you have you any brothers or sisters Jo?
S	A sister.
C	What's her name?
S	Heather, she plays the drums.

C	That's great. Joanne look at me, don't fall asleep.
S	No, I won't.
C	Do you like this shirt?
S	It's nice yes.
C	Um, do, do you come here often?
S	No.
C	Neither do I. Where's that brandy?
N	I don't know.
C	Have, have I seen you before?
S	I don't think so.
C	Don't fall asleep.
S	I won't.
C	What's your favourite drink?
S	Tea.

[A enters with a mug of tea]

C	Where've you been?
A	Sorry there was a queue.
N	Never mind, better late than never aye Joanne? Mmm that looks delicious Wendy, thank you. *[Takes tea]* Mmm.
C	Oi.
A	Hold on.
N	Oh yes very refreshing. Do you want some Joanne? Aye? *[Taunts S with the tea]*
C	That's hers.
A	I brought it for her.
N	Will you leave this to me. Do you want a lovely cup of tea Joanne? A lovely refreshing cuppa aye? Mmmm delicious.
C	Stop drinking her tea!
A	If you want it you should get your own.
N	Look, this is my department will you just give me a chance. Mmm! Oh I'm parched this is delicious. Do you want some Joanne?
S	Yes please.
C	Well give her it then!
N	Look I can't give it to her, I'm torturing her.
C	That's not very nice.
N	Of course it's not very nice, it's torture, it's not supposed to be nice!

C   I spent ages bringing her back from the brink the least you can do is/

N   Well, well done, good for you.

C   Pleasure.

N   Wendy slaps her about, you bring her round, now I put the squeeze on. For the tape the witness is taking refreshment. *[She's not]* Mmm do you want a cup of tea Joanne?
[Improvisation as N taunts S with tea]

C   That'll never work.

N   Okay that's it, you do it! Come on, you try. It's not as easy as it looks.
[C takes the mug]
That's it, you waft it around under her nose.

A   It'll be cold now anyway.

N   That's it.

C   What do I ask her?

N   "Do you want a cup of tea?"

C   Is that it?

N   Just get on with it. "Do you want a cup of tea?"

C   Do you want a cup of tea?

N   What's that "Do you want a cup of tea?"

C   That's how you do it.

N   No it's not!

C   It is, you put on a stupid voice.

N   I don't. Do it in a proper voice.

C   Do you want a cup of tea?

N   *[Imitating C]* "Do you want a cup of tea?"

C   What's the matter with you?

N   That's how you do it.

C   No I don't!

N   Try it again.

C   As long as you don't take the piss.

N   No, you're all right, come on.

C   Do you want a cup of tea?

N   That's it.

C   A lovely cup of tea.

N   That's it!

C   Oh it's nice and wet, do you want a sip.

S   Yes please.

N Fantastic, what no, no don't actually give her a sip! You don't actually let her drink it!
C Why not? She's thirsty.
N I know, I've been taunting her with it for days. I've drank gallons of the bloody stuff, I'm swilling and then you... unbelievable, bloody unbelievable!
A Will you two shut up! So, Joanne, now you're suitably refreshed, let's run through the facts as they stand shall we? Last night, *[insert yesterday's date]*, it's a cold night, foggy, you think about staying in to watch the big movie, it's a John Wayne feature, one of your favourites but at the last minute, for reasons that are yet to become clear, you decide to go out. Rather than risk taking a bus you decide to call a cab. At approximately nine o'clock you're delivered by cab to La Fourchette.
C A fashionable restaurant in Kings Cross.
A Accompanied by your boyfriend.
S House mate.
C Soul mate.
A Best mate.
N Shaun.
S A drummer with the local orchestra.
A Whatever.
C We've got the place wired.
N We know the chef, I could call him in if you wanted?
C That won't be necessary.
A At the next table we have our informant, a plumber called Dave.
C John.
A John, is eating at the next table with his wife.
N "Lovely food isn't it darling?"
A "Oh yes excellent and the service is good as well isn't it?"
N "So it should be at these prices"
A "You get what you pay for"
   [This banal domestic conversation continues improvised until C decides to cut it off]
C This Mr. Kennedy identifies two friends who join you as Heather and Mark, the park attendants.
A "Did you see the snooker last night?"

C	"No I wanted to but you wanted to watch the movie on the other side didn't you love?"
S	"Yeah"
C	"Did you see it?"
A	"No, we got our furniture repossessed"
S	"I don't believe it!"
A	"Yeah, Darren's got us into serious debt haven't you love?"
N	"I rather not talk about it."
A	"Holidays in Barbados, the works!"
S	"Is that true?"
A	"Yeah"
C	"You should cut down on the luxuries"
S	"And the fats"
C	"You're porking out a bit"
S	"I think he's nice like that"
N	"Like what?"
C	"A bit porky"
N	"I'm not porky. Am I porky?"
S	"No, he's not porky"
C	"So what's your idea of porky?"
S	"It's not about weight is it"
N	"It's about how people carry themselves"
S	"Exactly!"
C	"But do you think he's attractive like that?"
S	"Well what do you think?"
C	"Don't ask me?"
S	Sound familiar?
A	Yes it does.
C	That's it! We've got you banged to rights Joanne, don't try any funny stuff. Raise your right hand. Hold this *[mug]*, do you deny that this is anything but a true and fair representation of the events of last night?
A	No.
S	And do you have anything to add?
N	The witness is shaking her head. *[She's not]*
S	Any more questions?
C	No.
N	No.
S	*[To A]* In that case you can go.

N	She has to sign the form.
S	Oh yes.
C	What's this?
A	A pen.
C	So use it.
S	Could you sign the form Joanne?
A	Where?
C	At the bottom.
A	Okay.
C	W. A. T. T.
N	Oh right! Watt actually is her name!
S	Bye.
A	Bye
	[A has got up to go but looks lost]
N	Joanne, do you know where you're going?
A	No.
S	62 Walford Road.
N	Drive.
C	*[Giving A pages from the interrogator's sketch book]* This is your house. This is Shaun. This is you, you smile a lot. Actually you may as well take the lot. *[Gives A the notebook]*
A	Thank You.
	[A cautiously leaves the theatre through the auditorium]

[As the lights fade C, N & S are seen coming together discussing what has just happened as newsreaders used to at the end of the TV news]

Original Programme Notes

Stan's Cafe

Good and True

devised and performed by

Sarah Dawson
Amanda Hadingue
Craig Stephens
Nick Walker

direction James Yarker

lighting Paul Arvidson
sound Brian Duffy
design Stan's Cafe

administration Paulette Brien
photography Ed Dimsdale
graphics Simon Ford

with thanks to Neil Robson, Blast Theory, Denise Gilfoyle, MAC, DanceXchange, Stephen Downing, the Stan's Cafe board: Katherine Anderson, Jaki Booth, Rob Elkington, David Sefton, Gwen Van Spijk and Mole Wetherell. Our friends at West Midlands Arts and Birmingham City Council who have made this show possible.

Good and True is about asking questions. It is about the motivations, tactics, revelations and assumptions embedded in questioning. It is about the troubled relationship between questions and answers. Except in the loosest possible sense it is not a story, though it can be found to contain fragments of many stories.

It is always exciting and frightening working on Stan's Cafe shows. They are made in the rehearsal room by trying theoretical ideas out in practice, using instinct and chance as well as tough thinking, so it's difficult to predict what form the final performance will take. It turns out that *Good and True*, in contrast to most recent projects, is based almost entirely on dialogue.

Despite the abundance of text there is no writer's credit. Much of this text is the result of improvisations by the cast which have been transcribed then edited, rewritten, rehearsed, edited and rewritten again. Other passages have been written from scratch by me according to speech patterns and themes brought into currency through improvisation. There remain a few passages which are improvised afresh with each performance. In such circumstances authorship is clearly shared.

Ultimately, the show is not yet finished – it remains open for you to do your own writing job on it. We know why everything in the show is there but we haven't nailed down what everything means. The creative links you make within the show and the meaning you draw from it will complete our collaboration.

James Yarker
February 2000

Some Questions Tell Their Own Lies.

This is an early sketch for *Good and True*. We recorded it 'on location' in a meeting room at West Midlands Arts and in an attempt to sound like a recording from a police interrogation room used the longest takes we could manage.

I wrote the script inspired by Donald Barthelme's brilliant short story, *Concerning The Bodyguard*. The recording forms part of the Stan's Cafe CD *Pieces for the Radio* (volume 1).

> Al Heely = Female Police Sargent
> Valentine = Male Police Sargent
> Bowen = Male Police Sargent
> Jo Chamberlain = Female Suspect

To be recorded in a sparely furnished, uncarpeted room. Action implied by the text is to be physically acted out during recording. The sound quality is to be that of a police interview room evidence tape.

Al	Three minutes past four, Tuesday 14th July, 1998. Interview Room 4. Present: Sergeants Valentine and Heely. Are you Jo Chamberlain of Flat 4, 12 Republic Square?
Jo	I am.
Al	Miss Chamberlain we don't want to detain you longer than necessary so if you can answer a few questions relating to the events of last night then we can all get on.
Jo	Okay.
Al	First up, can you tell us were you were between 9pm and 2am on the night of the thirteenth?
Jo	I was in my flat.
Al	For that whole time?
Jo	Yes.
Al	And you didn't go out?
Jo	No.

Al	Were you with anyone who could confirm this for us?
Jo	No, I'm sorry.
Al	Did you see any neighbours on your way in or out?
Jo	No.
Al	Did you call anyone?
Jo	No, no I don't think so.
Val	Did you see the film on TV?
Jo	I'm sorry?
Val	The film. The big film. Did you watch the TV?
Jo	No.
Al	Do you have a partner Ms.Chamberlain?
Jo	No.
Al	So you live alone?
Jo	Yes.
Al	And you're pretty self contained, you don't need company?
Val	Even last night.
Al	Last night, tell us what happened.
Jo	I was at home, I was reading.
Al	What?
Jo	A novel.
Al	What?
Jo	Just trash.
Val	You were taking your mind off things?
Jo	No I wasn't, I was just reading.
Al	You were just reading?
Val	And you took a trip to the refrigerator and you made yourself coffee.
Al	Do you always make yourself coffee?
Val	You poison yourself on the stuff. You keep no alcohol in the place and you jack yourself up with caffeine and read trash fiction through the night and you never leave the house.
Al	I don't think so!
Val	You're a beautiful lady.
Al	Very.
Val	And you must have admirers.
Al	Many.
Val	And if you want company you have plenty of numbers to call.
Al	Sure.
Val	So last night you didn't need anyone, you didn't speak to

	anyone, you didn't contact anyone.
Al	Or maybe one person?
Jo	No, no one.
Al	You need someone now, someone to back you up. If you don't have anyone fighting for you then it's your word a/
	[Door opens and closes]
Val	Inspector Bowen has entered the room.
Al	...it's your word and nothing more. You need someone as an alibi. Was there really no one?
Jo	No
Val	Help yourself Jo, say who it was and we'll leave you alone.
Bo	You're seen Ms.Chamberlain. You're seen watching in bars, you're seen smiling, you're seen dancing with strange men. You drink and you smile and you pass the time. You've been seen with a book in your hand scribbling, you take notes and you stare out. We met once, do you remember? In a bar down town, dark wood, no jukebox, crowded. You talked about leaving the city, having no ties, finishing your contract and flying off. You wouldn't let me buy you a drink, do you remember?
Jo	No.
Bo	You remember my face though. I told you about my job. I seemed vague. I was making it up as I went along. You smiled a lot, you nodded a lot.
Jo	No.
Val	We saw it, we were sitting at the next table, we couldn't hear you but we read your body language. You were open, flirtatious, we read it from your body. You were saying how you had lost faith in art as a means of questioning, that you didn't believe in anything anymore but direct action and you said that anyone who asked too many questions would lose any sense of what it was they were asking.
Bo	You smiled at me... you remember.
Jo	No.
Bo	You were plotting, behind those eyes, you were sparking plans. You wanted me, you remember, but I couldn't let myself, it would have blown my cover. I left abruptly. You remember?

Val	You were distraught.
	You called for more drinks, you treated the bar man as a confidante.
	You cried on a high stool and we read your crumpled posture. You cried about your lonely job and how everyone would only ever talk to you once, then walk away. You went home and took out a record but never played it, watched TV on mute and listened to the city below. You lay in bed but didn't sleep, read but didn't take in words. You were never seen again.
He	Do you remember now?
Jo	Maybe, but nothing like that.
Bo	Why did you do it?
Jo	What?
Bo	Who were you working with?
Jo	What?
Bo	Who are you covering for?
Jo	No one.
Bo	And you expect us to believe that? You've got history.
Jo	We've all got history.
Al	Do you recognise this?
Val	The suspect is being shown a rifle.
Jo	No.
Al	It was found in your flat.
Jo	I've never seen it before.
Al	It was found in your flat when we came to get you.
Jo	That's impossible!
Val	It was careless.
Jo	It's not mine.
Val	Then whose is it?
Jo	I've told you, I've never seen it before.
Val	Then why was it in your flat?
Jo	I don't know. I don't believe it.
Al	Neither did we. 'She can't be so stupid' we thought.
Bo	'What's she thinking of?' we thought.
Al	'She should have dumped this as soon as she used it'.
Bo	There's no point in holding onto it.
Al	It's incriminating evidence.

Bo	It's all we need Jo.
Al	Can you explain it away?
Bo	I've never seen it before!
Al	Then how did it get to be in your flat?
Bo	Someone must have hidden it there.
Al	When?
Bo	When I wasn't looking.
Al	When?
Bo	I don't know.
Al	When you were out?
Val	But you didn't go out!
Al	When your friend came round?
Val	But you had no friends round!
Jo	It's impossible!
Val	Maybe, but unless you can tell us who put it there you're in the frame.
Jo	This is a set up.
Al	You mean a fit up.
Jo	Whatever.
Al	Is there anyone who has access to your flat except you?
Jo	No.
Al	And there's no set of spare keys?
Jo	No.
Val	So you trust yourself.
Al	Has anyone else held your keys? Could anyone have got duplicates made?
Bo	Are you protecting anyone?
Jo	No.
Bo	You're in the frame Jo.
Jo	I know.
Bo	So tell us a name.
Al	*[Quietly]* Make one up.
Jo	No, I'm not scared.
Bo	Have you given anyone cause to hate you?
Jo	Probably.
Bo	Give it up Jo.
Jo	You can't not hurt people can you?
Al	Give us a reason to cross you off the list Jo.
Jo	I didn't do whatever it is you think I've done.

Al   What do you think we think you've done Jo?
Jo   I don't know and I don't know why you won't tell me.

Bo   You lay there, it was still smoking in your hand and you watched all the chaos playing out in a distanced slow motion. You saw your action and all the ricocheting reaction and you wondered numbly, "how can I have detonated all that with my simple action and how could I, with all the best intentions, have cause all that havoc? Surely this is a clean thing I have done, a simple answer to so many questions. I'm looking down on them and they're all looking out for me and they've all got their stories now and I'm at the heart of them all. I am the answer to so many questions". You think about the gun.
[There are series of crashes that continue into the next passage]

Al   The suspect has hit the table with her fist several times.
Val   You're angry, losing it and your powers are fading and we love you. We want to care for you, but you won't let us close. You shake all good things in your life to bits, fall through the net, fail to connect and don't say the words. You won't give it up and fail to say what you mean. We love you, but you won't let us close. You're our answer and you'll never fade from our minds. We're drowning and you've not written in years and there are never any messages and we've been bugging you and your home but you never mutter our names in the night. You never say anything unguarded about us and you never even mention us. If we didn't know better we'd think you never thought of us.
Al   The suspect is asleep.
Bo   What was she wearing last night?
Al   A ball gown.
Bo   She was at the ball.
Al   It was a silver gown, skimming the floor.
Bo   They were both there, white and silver gowns off the shoulder.
Al   They were giggling behind fans, rustling. Make up and long gloves.
Bo   Chaste kisses, masks, dances.

Al	Fans, corsets and gallant men.
Bo	Fops.
Al	Bows and bustles, games of intrigue, flirtations, bons mots and veiled insults.
Bo	Double talk and high fashion and dancing partners.
Al	Marked cards, an orchestra and "would you care to dance" and "no thank you, I'm quite, quite exhausted!"
Bo	Courteous gestures hiding spiteful jealousy.
Al	Perfume and pistols at dawn.
Val	Discarded corpses and a ransacked room.
Bo	Four poster beds and a long way home and corridors and curtains flapping in the wind.
Al	And rapiers pricked with blood and deeply held hatreds and stripped to the waist and screaming drunk and "she's killed him!"
Val	"She's killed him".
Al	And "he never would have known".
Val	Spilled wax, heavy drapes.
Al	Laudanum.
Val	And opium and fantastic visions and silhouettes.
Bo	And "I've loved you all these years!"
Al	And deaths in childbirth.
Bo	She should never have gone away.
Val	Trees, clipped hedges, water features.
Bo	And some other man.
Al	Infidelity, infatuation, infanticide, fantasies, locked attic rooms, deeply held lust and "never let go. keep hold of me". Clasped on the terrace. Full moon, skimming clouds: silhouettes of avenues of trees and lead roofs and gargoyles and brandy and port and no sense of history. "She loves me". "She's killed him". "It's night-time".
Val:	And the suspect sleeps on.
Al:	Great.
Val:	So why didn't you call?
Al:	I've told you.
Val:	So tell me again.
Al:	I was busy .
Val:	But you got the message?
Al	Sure.

Val:	So you knew how urgent it was?
Al:	I was busy.
Val:	Sure.
Bo:	Jo, forget them.
Al:	I was, I can't always drop everything.
Val:	But you could have called, forget the machine.
Al:	Do you need it spelt out? I was busy.
Val:	Doing what?
Bo:	Forget everything around us.
Al:	Working.
Val:	On what.
Bo:	Forget outside.
Al:	The usual, what do you think?
Val:	Pardon?
Bo:	Forget last night.
Al:	What else could I have been doing?
Val:	I don't know.
Bo:	Forget the bruises.
Al:	No? What do you think I was doing?
Val:	Nothing.
Bo:	Forget the hunger.
Al:	But I was doing something wasn't I? What were you imagining?
Bo:	Forget the time.
Val:	I don't know.
Al:	I don't believe you!
Bo:	Forget your tiredness, forget history, forget the future, forget consequences. Look into my eyes, look at me, look at me. Tell me what you see.
Jo:	You.
Bo:	Who?
Jo:	Just you, you know.
Bo:	And who am I?
Jo:	I don't know.
Val	Did you let them touch you?
Jo	Yes.
Val	*[Quietly]* Shit.
Al	Why?
Jo	They needed me.

Al	They needed to feel you?
Jo	Yes.
Al	So... so what happened?
	Did they lean on you? Into you? Did they cover your hands in their hands, their arms round your arms, their chests on your shoulders. They guided your hands, cutting meat, drawing signs, signing documents, under duress.
Val	They guided your hands over their bodies.
Al	Their warmth, your warmth.
Jo	They needed me.
Al	They touched you.
Jo	And so you let them hold you.
Bo	Who?
Jo	I can't say.
Val:	Do you recognise these faces?
Al:	The suspect is being shown photographs.
Val:	No? No? Surely this one? Not in the least? Are any of these familiar?
Al:	The suspect is shaking her head.
Val	They must look familiar. It was a crowd, someone must have looked a bit like this.
Jo	I've only seen you.
Val:	But we're not them, we're us.
Bo:	What he means is, we're the police.
Val:	We do the investigating, we investigate them. Before you saw us you must have seen them. It was a busy night, there were people all over, on all the streets, the place was swarming, you must have seen someone.
Jo:	I didn't go out.
Val:	You looked out the window, you looked out from behind your curtains, through the window down on the rioters, at these people.
Jo	I didn't look out, I've only seen you.
Val:	I can't believe that.
Bo:	Ms.Chamberlain what were you doing last night between 9pm & 2am?
Jo:	I was thinking about questions and how they twist the answers they seek.
Bo:	And you were doing this all night?

Jo: Yes.
Bo: That's a lot of thinking.
Jo: There were other things to think about.
Bo: Like?
Jo: Like – why do people ask questions they already know the answer to? Why do people ask questions when they know answers will only hurt them? Why/
Bo   You like thinking about questions?
Jo   You like asking questions?
Bo: I ask the questions.
Jo: But do you like it?
Al: He asks the questions.
Jo: So do you.
Al: Right.
Jo: So?
Val: So you keep a low profile, you coordinate it all but you keep your distance. You don't get involved in the action, build an alibi, spend the night somewhere else, with respected respectable people, police officers perhaps, us for example. You should have come out with us, we'd have shown you a good time, kept you out of that kind of trouble at least.
Bo&Al: Shut up!
Val: What?
Al: You know.
Val: I didn't say anything!
Al: You always say something and it's always too much.
Val: I don't.
Al: You do, you always do, you fantasise, it gets us into trouble.
Val: She's provocative.
Bo: This is going on the record.
Val: *[Quietly]* Shit.
        Ms.Chamberlain what are you doing here?
Jo   You brought me here.
Val: I know, but why?
Jo: You wanted to ask me questions.
Val: What questions?
Jo: You wanted me to listen to you.
Val: You wouldn't be here if you didn't know something.
Jo: You wanted me to nod and cry and say sorry and make you

	out to be brave and righteous and pious and you are, sometimes. And here I am for you, to listen and to answer your questions.
Bo:	Where were you?
Jo:	With you.
Bo:	What were you doing?
Jo:	Holding you.
Bo:	And?
Jo:	kissing you.
Bo:	And ?
Jo:	Talking to you.
Bo:	About?
Jo:	About how some questions tell their own lies.
Al:	So that's where you were?
Bo:	Yes.
Val:	While we were outside?
Bo:	Yes.
Jo:	While you were hitting the prefect?
Al:	Yes.
Jo:	Why did you do that?
Al:	Because it was the only answer.
Jo:	And you've got no more questions?
Al:	No, not many.
Jo:	Interview ends.
Val:	We say that.
Jo:	Then say it.
Val:	Interview ends.

[Silence, then end of tape hiss]

James Yarker, 1998

About the illustration and design

The illustrations for the covers of these books were undertaken by students at Birmingham City University as the final module of their first-year illustration course during the Spring/Summer of 2018. The images were developed through workshops using variations of the theatre-devising methods employed by Stan's Cafe but adapted and applied to the making of visual work. The resulting work was shown in the pop-up exhibition *The Something Of Somebody Something* at Stan's Cafe's venue @AE Harris in May 2018.

The design concept of the books was produced by final year Graphic Design student Aimee Chapman. These were then further developed for print in a collaborative process between Stan's Cafe and the University's Innovation Product Support Service (IPSS) which involved helping the company to select appropriate DTP software, undertaking training and selecting a suitable print on demand service.

Gareth Courage
Lecturer in Illustration
Birmingham City University

www.ingramcontent.com/pod-product-compliance
Lightning Source LLC
Chambersburg PA
CBHW070104120526
44588CB00034B/2254